ENHANCING COMMITTEE EFFECTIVENESS

Handbook for Committee Chairs, Staff Liaisons, and Committee Members

REVISED EDITION

JOHN F. SCHLEGEL, PharmD, MSEd, CAE

In this publication, the term "committee" applies to standing committees, task forces, ad hoc committees, councils, commissions, or any working group.

Although developed for the community of professional, trade, philanthropic associations and other not-for-profit entities, the contents of this publication provide an invaluable guide to anyone who is chairing a committee or simply chairing a meeting, no matter what the setting.

The Center for Association Leadership

WASHINGTON, D.C.

The author has worked diligently to ensure that all information in this book is accurate as of the time of publication and consistent with standards of good practice in the general management community. As research and practice advance, however, standards may change. For this reason it is recommended that readers evaluate the applicability of any recommendations in light of particular situations and changing standards.

ASAE: The Center for Association Leadership
1575 I Street, NW
Washington, DC 20005-1103
Phone: (202) 626-2723; (888) 950-2723 outside the metropolitan Washington, DC
  area
Fax: (202) 220-6439
Email: books@asaecenter.org
We connect great ideas and great people to inspire leadership and achievement in the association community.

Keith C. Skillman, CAE, Vice President, Publications, ASAE: The Center for Association
  Leadership
Baron Williams, CAE, Director of Book Publishing, ASAE: The Center for Association
  Leadership

Cover and interior design by Troy Scott Parker, Cimarron Design

This book is available at a special discount when ordered in bulk quantities. For information, contact the ASAE Member Service Center at (202) 371-0940.

A complete catalog of titles is available on the ASAE: The Center for Association Leadership website at asaecenter.org.

Published by Association Management Press, an imprint of ASAE: The Center for Association Leadership

ISBN-13: 978-0-88034-314-5
ISBN-10: 0-88034-314-1

Printed in the United States of America.

10 9 8 7 6 5 4 3

CONTENTS

THE
COMMITTEE

If the board of directors is the "brain" of
an association, committees are the central
nervous system. When they operate well,
they accurately sense the environment,
process information, and provide valuable
guidance to the "brain" so that it can
make good decisions. When they do not
operate well, the association suffers.

Types of Committees

An association is governed by a volunteer board of directors; committees are established to assist in this governance. *Management committees,* which are defined in the bylaws, have specific memberships and continuing assignments from year to year. *Standing committees* are designated to make policy recommendations to the board, to undertake long-term assignments, and to carry out the work of the association. *Task forces, ad hoc committees* and other special working groups are most often formed by the governing board or the chief elected officer to undertake highly focused tasks within a specific period of time, usually one year or less.

In recent years most effective and successful associations have recognized the importance of minimizing bureaucracy, streamlining and accelerating decision-making, and using association financial and human resources more strategically. To accomplish this, there has been a trend toward having only a minimum number of Standing Committees and Management Committees, and to increasingly use ad hoc committees and task forces. These latter two are appointed to accomplish much more focused tasks within specific time frames. Use of ad hoc committees and task forces allows associations to be much more nimble, to impose much more accountability, and to create a culture of doing work in a manner that is more competitive with today's highly competitive business environment. Use of more ad hoc committees and fewer standing committees also creates more opportunities for volunteer participation in the association and thus a greater sense of affiliation and loyalty to the association and its work. Recent research studies, *The Decision to Volunteer* and *The Decision to Join,* undertaken and published by ASAE & The Center for Association Leadership, found that an engaged member or volunteer was more apt to remain a member and positively promulgate the benefits of association membership. Finally, volunteers are generally much more motivated to participate in working groups with very specific tasks to accomplish in specific time frames. This approach provides greater assurance that their time is being used wisely and that the expertise they bring to the group is valued.

Establishment of Committees

Appointment Process

Each year the chair of the board of directors appoints the leadership, and sometimes the entire membership, of standing and special committees of the association. Often the leadership of these important committees is ratified by the entire board. Recent committee chairs, the committee's staff liaison, and other relevant staff and volunteer leaders should be consulted when selecting the committee chair and members of the committee. Because associations are so dependent upon the quality of products or services and recommendations coming from these member working groups, competency in the committee's area of responsibility is an important requirement for the committee chair and all members of the committee. Another important consideration is diversity in the makeup of committees, taking into consideration age, gender, geography, and ethnicity, as well as making certain that there is good representation of the various segments of the membership.

The term of service for a committee member usually is one year, renewable up to three years. The chair is generally selected from the previous year's committee membership and generally serves in this leadership position for one year. In today's environment of rapid change, it is critical that committee membership and leadership is refreshed each year with new perspectives and new thinking brought in by the appointment of new people. The tradition in many associations of very long term service on a committee by a select few is giving way to this new thinking.

Purpose of Committees

Associations are built on a system of committee actions, linking the association with the attitudes, expectations and needs in the real world of its members. Committees represent, involve, and serve members. They also provide an important training ground for future leaders. Committees are an effective workforce for the association—they ensure group participation in problem solving and provide a critical forum for the many interests within the association.

Effective committees unify, represent, motivate, coordinate, consolidate, and communicate. They function best when their members are selected appropriately and they have a clearly defined mission, strong leadership, and competent staffing.

Committee Administration

Chair and staff liaison. The committee chair and staff liaison, working in partnership, are responsible for facilitating the work of the committee, providing oversight, and ensuring timely communications within the committee and between the committee and other components of the association. The staff liaison also provides logistical support for the committee's work.

Board liaison. Some associations have a board member who sits on the committee and serves as its liaison to the board. This person is a leadership resource person for the committee chair and staff liaison and a resource to the board regarding the committee's activities. Board liaisons must be careful not to overly influence committees, since the association is looking for the committee to provide fresh, new perspective and thinking. The board liaison should focus on being primarily a communication link between board and committee.

Committee reports. The committee chair and staff are responsible for keeping leadership and appropriate staff fully informed of committee activities. A written report of goals and achievements should be provided to the board of directors at least two or three times a year.

Committee charge. In addition to the general committee charge, which outlines the committee's scope of activity, the board of directors or board chair may charge the committee with specific work. The committee chair and staff liaison are responsible for keeping the work of the committee focused on the charge and aligned with the association's strategic plan. At the conclusion of each year, the chair and staff liaison are expected to make recommendations to the board and chief staff executive of the association regarding future work of the committee.

Committee responsibilities. Committees are directly responsible to the board of directors through the office of the chief staff executive.

Committees may not commit to expenditure of funds and may not express opinions or represent positions in the name of the association unless specifically authorized by the board. If proposing a program or activity that may involve expenditure of funds, committees must submit a program description and budget to the chief staff executive for inclusion in the association budget that must be approved by the board before undertaking the program or activity.

Reports. The committee chair and staff liaison are responsible for keeping committee members fully informed with timely reports of all committee meetings and committee work conducted by telephone conference and written communications. A "Sample Committee Report" form (see page 33) should be completed by the committee chair and staff liaison before all board meetings, or at least 2-3 times a year.

Meetings. To economize on the financial and personal time cost of meetings, committees often set meetings to occur in conjunction with other association meetings. This works well so long as sufficient time is set aside for committees to conduct their work. It is increasingly popular for committees to meet throughout the year via teleconference. This is an effective way of doing work in a timely manner. It is also a useful way to take care of routine matters so that limited on-site meeting time is used effectively to tackle issues better dealt with when the committee is working in the more interactive setting of a face-to-face meeting.

Member responsibilities. Members are expected to fully participate in committee activities by attending meetings and conducting business by telephone and written communications. Members are expected to:

- Act in good faith and in the best interest of the association, not on behalf of their own personal interest or even that of a constituency group of which they feel a part.
- Take on responsibilities and commit to fulfilling them in a timely manner.
- Disclose real or perceived conflicts of interest, and refrain from voting in these instances.
- Refrain from discussions or activities that may violate antitrust laws.

THE EFFECTIVE
COMMITTEE CHAIR

The following checklists are
quick references to help the
committee chair lead his/her committee.

COMMITTEE CHAIR
POSITION DESCRIPTION

BASIC FUNCTION

Consistent with the association's policy and strategic plan, the committee chair guides the committee in its work as outlined by the scope of work and charge from the chief elected officer and board of directors.

RESPONSIBILITIES

- With staff, develop a work plan that will allow the committee to effectively and efficiently discharge its responsibilities for the year.
- With staff, develop agendas and conduct committee meetings.
- Approve reports of committee meetings before their distribution.
- Work with staff to ensure that the work of the committee is carried out between meetings.
- Approve reports on committee activities, including requests to the board of directors for action.
- Report to the committee on decisions of the board of directors or executive committee that affect the committee's work or activities.
- Where appropriate, guide the committee in proposing products and services that will further the goals and objectives of the association.
- Where appropriate, make policy recommendations to the board of directors.

Effectively Chairing a Committee— A Demanding Role

Challenges Facing Committee Chairs

- Decreasing volunteer time.
- Increasing expectations by members.
- Demand to use association resources more strategically.
- Increasing expectations of committee performance.

Committee Leadership is More than Chairing a Meeting, It Involves

- Preparing for meetings—don't meet until you are prepared to use people's time effectively.
- How you conduct the meeting—administratively and substantively.
- Effective facilitation of all discussions—*assuring inclusiveness and full participation.*
- Keeping the committee productive between meetings.
- Motivating people to participate and creating buy-in at meetings and throughout the year.

Effective Committee Chairs Must

- Motivate people to participate.
- Chair meetings effectively.
- Assure committee performance.

Reduced Volunteer Time: The New Reality

When asking members to volunteer, associations and committee chairs must:

- Value their time—reduce your demands on their time; assure *strategic* use of their time.
- Value and recognize their contribution—what's the unique value they add?
- Understand and respond to their need for positive reinforcement for their participation.

Qualities of the Effective Committee Chair

COMMUNICATION SKILLS

- Demonstrates ability to communicate with committee members, staff, and other groups.
- Demonstrates willingness to listen (communication is *not* necessarily talking).

PARTICIPATION

- Demonstrates active participation and interest in the association.
- Commands prestige and respect from within the industry or profession.
- Has knowledge of the subject in which the committee is involved.
- Thinks in terms of association goals.

LEADERSHIP

- Commands attention and inspires others.
- Demonstrates ability to create a positive work atmosphere.
- Controls without dominating.
- Understands how the committee fits in to the larger work of the association.

ADMINISTRATIVE SKILLS

- Demonstrates willingness to take the initiative.
- Demonstrates ability and willingness to carry out responsibilities and complete work in a timely manner.
- Supports orderly procedures for conducting work.
- Embraces the importance of engaging most/all committee members in the committee's work.
- Understands the "partnership" role of the staff.

Responsibilities of the Chair

- Attend and actively chair all meetings.
- Accept and support the committee's charge.
- Plan committee meetings and agendas with staff.
- Exercise leadership within and outside the committee.
- Maintain records and relevant information on committee work. Be sufficiently informed to interact knowledgeably with other committee members, staff, and others outside the committee.
- Move members toward active participation, decision making, and achieving consensus.
- Continually evaluate committee efforts and communicate accomplishments to the committee, association leadership, and the membership.

Making Early Contact With Committee Members

- Within two weeks of appointments, send a welcome/orientation letter, cosigned by the committee staff liaison or at least identifying this staff contact.
- Provide the committee with its charges and goals, always in the context of the association's strategic plan. Show how the committee's work fits into the big picture.
- Provide the date and location of the first meeting and best estimate of how frequently the committee will meet in face-to-face meetings and/ or conference calls throughout the year.
- Review recent accomplishments of the committee so that the work to be done can be put into context.
- Provide a "Committee Member Position Description" (see page 38) which includes a list of committee member responsibilities.
- Include an RSVP sheet for committee participation and for attendance at the committee meeting if the date is set. Some chairs may wish to solicit agenda items. If this is done, remember that the first requirement of a committee is to fulfill the charge provided to it by the association.

Developing and Structuring the Meeting Agenda

- Never hold a meeting without an agenda sent out in advance. You can't expect responsible participation when people do not have time to prepare.

- Work closely with the staff liaison in developing the agenda for the meeting.

- Provide an agenda sheet that lists all the agenda items to be taken up, but also the following basic information: the start and ending times for the meeting; the meeting room number; and a list of committee members (those expected to attend and those expected to be absent).

- Sequence agenda items thoughtfully. Committee meetings are like any team sport. The group needs to "warm up" together before tackling the tougher work. Therefore, start the meeting with agenda topics that will unify the committee; this sets the stage for working together. Early in the meeting, when people are fresh, is a good time to discuss topics that require mental energy, creativity, and clear thinking. Do not put difficult topics back-to-back—people need a break. Also, do not put difficult or controversial items at the end of a meeting, when people are tired and less likely to tolerate difficult discussions. Make the first few topics after lunch quick-action items to create positive momentum at a time when people are often lethargic from eating. Build in breaks at logical places in the agenda, at least every two hours. End the meeting with topics that will unify the committee; people like to leave meetings feeling that they are part of a productive team. This also helps to create "buy-in" to the actions taken by the committee.

- Do not over-schedule the meeting. Provide sufficient but not too much time for each topic. Timed agendas are effective tools for managing a meeting. With a timed agenda, the estimated hour of the clock is noted preceding each agenda item (e.g. 1:45 p.m. immediately preceding agenda item #1; 2 p.m. immediately preceding agenda item #2.) Show the times for breaks and lunch. Placing these "markers" on the agenda sheet lets members know the general pace of discussion the chair anticipates for the meeting. It is surprising how effective a tool this is for helping to keep discussions focused, and for others on the committee helping the chair stay on schedule.

- Provide at least minimal written background information for each agenda item.
- Identify the person who is presenting each agenda item.

Being an Effective Facilitator of Discussions

- Be a facilitator of meetings; don't "hold court." The committee belongs to the association, not to the chair.

- Guide, mediate, probe, draw people in and stimulate discussions. Committees are not formed to simply validate the thinking of the chair or staff, so it is the responsibility of the chair to encourage broad participation to bring new ideas, thoughts and solutions into the discussion.

- Encourage a clash of ideas, but not of personalities. Good decisions result when a committee examines all sides of an issue. Don't let members personalize the debate and don't let one or two members dominate the discussion. Emotional discussion of an idea is good, but an emotional reaction to a person is bad. When emotions are too high, return the floor to a neutral person, seek a purely factual answer, or take a break.

- Prevent one-sided discussions. As chair you are responsible for making sure that discussions are balanced, no matter what your personal beliefs.

- Deal with people who are being difficult. Don't let a person who is blocking constructive discussion ruin the committee meeting for everyone else. If necessary, call for a break and talk privately with the person causing difficulty, calling attention to how this is counterproductive to constructive discussion. Perhaps suggest an alternate way in which the person can make his/her point.

- Keep discussions on track; periodically summarize and refocus the discussion, reminding people of the goal of the discussion.

- Monitor participation, control talkative members and draw silent members into the discussion. There is no point in people attending a meeting and yet not participating in discussions. If members don't participate, why attend?

- Use well-placed questions, seek points of information and clarification, and periodically summarize to keep the discussion focused.

- Be sensitive to the feelings of members. Look for visual and verbal cues to determine if a member is not happy with the discussion, and then deal with his or her discomfort during a break if possible.
- Keep the group focused on the central question and moving toward a decision. Call on the least senior members first to express their views; discussions tend to "close down" after senior members express strong views.
- Meetings should not just validate the thinking of the chair, staff, or one or two dominant people.
- Seek consensus—a decision that all members will support even though they may not agree with every little detail. Committees do not need unanimous agreement. Sometimes a good idea is badly compromised by trying to get every last person to completely agree.
- Close the meeting by
  - Noting achievements and focusing on positive outcomes of the meeting.
  - Confirming assignments and due dates.
  - Confirming understanding of next steps on major issues.
  - Reinforcing the importance of wide participation in committee deliberations.
  - Saying "thanks."

Tips for Presiding Over a Meeting

- Open the meeting on time. To do otherwise is disrespectful of those who came on time.
- Do a brief overview of the business to be conducted.
- Recognize members who are entitled to talk; discourage interruptions.
- If members are participating via phone connection in face-to-face meetings, regularly invite them into discussions and confirm with them regarding their opinions or votes on all issues.
- Restate the issue to be voted on and explain the consequences of the vote prior to calling for the vote.
- Put all issues to a fair vote. Don't make assumptions about how committee members feel or simply pass over a decision by saying something like "I think we all agree."

- Announce the results of actions taken and explain the follow-through to be taken and by whom.
- Help expedite business. Don't let discussions drift, get repetitive, or go on too long.
- Stay with the agenda. Seek the full committee's agreement to change the agenda once it has been announced.
- Close the meeting on time. Seek the committee's agreement regarding extending the time if necessary.

Parliamentary Procedure

- Committees are not required to operate using parliamentary procedure, with rare exceptions, such as when governing documents impose such a requirement. However, the objectives and principles of parliamentary procedure should be employed in all meetings.
- The objectives of parliamentary procedure include expediting business, maintaining order, ensuring justice and equity for all, and accomplishing the objectives for which the group is organized.
- The principles of parliamentary procedure include courtesy and justice to all, rule of the majority while respecting the rights of the minority, partiality to none, protection of the absentee, and taking one item of business at a time.

THE EFFECTIVE
STAFF LIAISON

The following checklists are
quick references to help the staff liaison
work with his/her committee.

STAFF LIAISON POSITION DESCRIPTION

BASIC FUNCTION

Serve as an informed resource person to the chair and members of the committee. Assist the chair in facilitating committee discussions and activities that address the committee's charge. Work with the chair to ensure that all committee work is consistent with the association's goals and objectives.

RESPONSIBILITIES

• Provide thorough orientation for each new committee chair, and assist the chair in providing orientation for new and continuing committee members each year.

• Work with the chair to develop a plan of work that will allow the committee to effectively and efficiently discharge its responsibilities for the year.

• Work with the chair to develop agendas and conduct effective meetings.

• Provide administrative support for planning and execution of all committee meetings.

• Draft reports of committee meetings for review and approval by the committee chair.

• Work with the chair, other committee members, and association staff to ensure that the work of the committee is carried forth between meetings.

• Facilitate communication of committee activities, including requests for action and/or proposed policies, to the chief staff executive and board of directors.

• Report to the committee chair and committee as a whole on decisions of the board of directors, executive committee, or other association committees which impact the committee's activities.

• Where appropriate, assist the committee in proposing products and services that will further the goals and objectives of the association.

The Role of the Staff Liaison

- Be a valuable resource to the committee, not simply a recording secretary. Note that too large a staff role reduces the value of the committee and reduces the motivation of volunteers. Too small a staff role often results in the committee's drifting aimlessly and operating ineffectively.

- Be thoroughly familiar with all aspects of the committee's work, including the scope of work, subjects under discussion, and association policies related to the committee's work.

- Answer questions, offer suggestions, and raise questions, but always do so by working through the chair.

- Provide administrative support to facilitate the work of the chair and committee members.

Responsibilities of the Staff Liaison to the Committee Chair

- Make early contact with the committee chair, if only with a phone call, within a week or two of his/her appointment.

- Provide a formal orientation program (see next section) soon after his/her appointment.

- Ensure that the chair executes his/her administrative duties.

- Maintain regular contact with the chair throughout the year, not only just before meetings.

- Provide administrative support to the committee throughout the year. The level of support should be agreed on by both the chair and staff liaison during the orientation of the chair.

- Help the chair prepare and distribute meeting agendas prior to the meeting.

- Help the chair prepare and distribute reports of committee meetings immediately following meetings.

- Provide on-site support for committee meetings.

- Help prepare committee reports to the board.

STAFF LIAISON

Orientation Program for the Chair by the Staff Liaison

(See "Committee Chair/Staff Liaison Partnership Agreement" on page 34.) If orientation cannot be done face-to-face, arrange for an hour phone call to allow plenty of time to cover all topics and reach a mutual understanding of roles and responsibilities. This early understanding is critical to working well together to expedite the work of the committee throughout the year. A typical orientation program includes the following elements:

- Create mutual understanding of the committee's work. Review the committee's charge and goals for the year and link them to the association's strategic plan. Review all ongoing committee projects and programs and the continuing assignments of individual committee members. Develop, working together with the chair, a program of work for the year (see "Committee Focus for the Year" on page 36).

- Identify the level of staff assistance available and make certain there is agreement on this up front.

- Clarify governance issues. Review and clarify the bounds of the committee's activity and authority. Review the association's bylaws and relevant association policies, practices, and procedures that affect the committee. Note where the work of other committees may overlap with or affect the committee.

- Clarify the chair's role and duties, and emphasize the importance of this position (see previous section, "The Effective Committee Chair").

- Clarify the role of staff liaison in relation to the chair.

- Determine the process to be used during the year for handling the committee's work. For example, agree on who will initiate the agenda preparation process and how soon agendas are to be sent out; who will initiate the preparation of minutes or meeting reports and how soon after meetings they are to be distributed; and how background materials will be put together.

- Provide the following background information in writing: a committee roster; minutes of previous committee meetings; a brief recap of recent committee activities and accomplishments; and a list of the board of directors, key staff, and other people with whom the chair is likely to interact.

FOR THE
COMMITTEE CHAIR
AND STAFF LIAISON

The following checklists help the
committee chair and staff liaison
work together to improve the
effectiveness of their committee.

Types of Committee Meetings and Communications

Committees are under increasing pressure to be productive on an ongoing basis, producing programs, products, services and recommendations throughout the year. Whereas in the past most committee business was accomplished in the occasional on-site meeting often coinciding with other association events, today's world of rapid change requires greater productivity on a more time sensitive basis. Today's committees use a combination of face-to-face meetings, conference call meetings, and emails to be productive throughout the year. This works well as long as the committee chair and staff liaison recognize that each of these formats has certain advantages and certain drawbacks.

• **Face-to-face meetings** are the most costly in terms of financial and human resources. They should be reserved for when it is important for the committee to tackle challenging or politically sensitive issues, where the group dynamic of being together with good eye contact is present, where the group can dig into a problem and then take breaks, and where private discussions can take place during breaks. This setting is also ideal for brainstorming ideas and dealing with subjects where spontaneity and creative thinking is needed. Face-to-face meetings should *not* be used to present routine reports or do other activities that can be done just as well "off line."

• **Conference call meetings** are an excellent means of conducting routine committee business and holding discussions or making decisions that do not demand the dynamics of face-to-face meetings. Conference call meetings often fail when the committee tries to tackle too much business on one call, or where highly complex or politically sensitive issues are undertaken. Sometimes this is necessary, but these types of discussions are always best handled in face-to-face meetings, and should only be undertaken in conference calls when absolutely necessary.

• **Emails** are an effective means of doing absolutely routine work, presenting background information, and keeping everyone informed. They can be used very effectively to "tee up discussions" for subsequent deliberation in conference calls or face-to-face meetings. Emails can often be used for taking quick votes on noncontroversial items, but they should not be used as "discussion forums." They can be used to generate ideas, but when attempts are made through emails to resolve complex issues, people often have a sense that they are being asked to rubber stamp someone else's idea. Also, decisions made through this process usually do not enjoy the same kind of continuing support that is true when decisions are reached through group discussion in conference calls or face-to-face meetings.

Face-to-Face Meetings

Room Setup and Seating

- Room setup and seating is critical to successful discussions.
- Set in a hollow square—not a long table with short ends and long sides.
- Seat 1/3 of participants per side of the hollow square.
- Seat only the chair and staff liaison at the remaining side of the hollow square.
- Eye contact between chair and all committee members is critical.
- Make certain there are tent cards with names and last minute handouts at each place.
- Make certain beverages are available and food, if appropriate. Confirm serving times with hotel staff.
- Creature comforts are very important—good lighting, room temperature, and lack of noise.

Before the Meeting Begins

- The committee chair and staff liaison should arrive early to check the room setup and reset the room if necessary. Also, place any last minute meeting materials at each place setting rather than incurring the disruption of handing out materials during discussions.
- Go over all agenda items one final time before the meeting begins so that you minimize surprises during the meeting.
- The staff liaison should sit next to the committee chair so that it is easy for him/her to discretely communicate with the chair as the meeting proceeds. The staff liaison should monitor participation by committee members and keep track of time to ensure that the meeting stays on schedule, that breaks are taken, that all members participate in the discussion, and that the meeting adjourns on time. Short hand notes

for the chair to view during discussions are invaluable tools that assist the chair in conducting the meeting effectively.

- Immediately after adjournment, the chair and staff liaison should meet briefly (preferably before leaving the meeting room) to agree on what follow-up actions are required, timelines, and who is responsible for each action (the chair, staff liaison, or another committee member).

Conducting Conference Call Meetings

Conference calls are now routinely used for meetings, yet few people think about the special challenges they present. Unlike face-to-face meetings, the chair does not have eye contact with all committee members, and committee members do not have eye contact among themselves. People cannot see the body language of others, which is a huge disadvantage both to the chair and to all committee members. Conference calls do not provide time during meeting breaks when some issues are talked through in private. Finally, conference calls do not provide the stimulus of personal contact that keep people alert during face-to-face meetings. Video conferencing or use of other computer-based video calls such as SKYPE attempt to bring into such calls the positive features of face-to-face meetings, such as eye contact and body language. As a practical matter, this occurs, and only with modest success, when using sophisticated videoconferencing equipment that is generally not available to most associations. As a practical matter, for at least the next several years, most association conference calls are likely to be telephone based and thus have the limitations noted above.

With all these thoughts in mind, the following guidelines will help to keep conference call meetings administratively and substantively productive.

- Use a toll free "call in" phone number; ask all members to call in two to three minutes before the meeting is scheduled to begin.

- Ask participants to press the "mute" button except when they want to speak. This is especially important if people are using speakerphones. Background noise can ruin a call, so deal with it.

- Keep the agenda very limited. Long calls with many agenda items are simply not productive. You may get through the agenda, but participants will feel little "buy-in" to decisions made, and feel more like they have been asked to agree to pre-determined decisions.

- Put out a detailed agenda in advance of the call. Because of the limitations of conference calls noted above, the agenda must provide much more detail to focus the discussion, even to the point of providing alternative possible decisions or courses of action. Without this focus, discussions tend to drift and one or two people tend to dominate discussion of each item.

- Include a roster of call participants as well as those not expected on the call. Because you do not have the visual cue of noting someone's absence, making note of committee members not on the call presents the opportunity for the chair or others to attempt to make sure the absent person's viewpoint, if it is known, is discussed. The chair has a special responsibility here.

- Limit the call to no more than one hour, or two at most. It is well documented that people's attention span drops dramatically after about 30 minutes on a phone call. You will have much more productive discussions if you schedule several one hour calls with limited agendas, than you will scheduling one long call.

- Start all calls on time by taking roll. Note who is not on the call and log them in as they join the call. Do not go back and restate the business conducted for late arrivals. This is disrespectful of those who were on time and wastes valuable time that should be spent in discussions.

- Advise people at the beginning of the call regarding how you plan to keep the discussion orderly.
  - Ask people to simply say their name if they wish to speak. This way the chair can keep a log of who is next up for the discussion.
  - Minimize "break-ins." If someone wishes to respond to a speaker, ask them to simply say their name and you will queue them up to speak in proper order.
  - Ask participants to keep their comments brief. It is very hard for people to track complex discussions on phone calls, so it is better to have people speak briefly in a focused manner, and then bring them back into the discussion after others have spoken if they have more to say.

- Use many of the same facilitation techniques discussed under "Being an Effective Facilitator of Discussions" (see page 17). It is particularly important during conference calls to not let one or two people dominate discussions. The chair must work especially hard at bringing all participants into the discussion, and to not let a long-winded speaker kill the discussion. This is the chair's responsibility and others on the call will appreciate the chair fulfilling those duties. Tell the speaker to wrap up in the next 15 seconds and you will come back to him/her later, which you may or may not do.

- Ask for a roll call vote on all decisions made. Silence does not necessarily convey agreement, and without positive voting many decisions on calls do not enjoy full support after the call has ended.

- Make certain that everyone understands the "next steps" to be taken after each decision.

- End the call on time. This is critical in keeping committee members feeling positive about conference call meetings. You are much better off terminating a call on time and scheduling another call to complete the remaining business than you are keeping the call going too long.

- Send a written report of the meeting and actions taken to the committee members *immediately* after the call. The dynamics of conference calls are such that people begin to remember differently both the discussions and decisions made on calls, more so than with face-to-face meetings.

Documenting the Results of Meetings— The Written Report

- Include the date, time, and place of the meeting. Note the chair's name, members present, and other key people in attendance.

- Note all formal motions and passage or defeat.

- Note all decisions reached, including motions passed and follow-up actions to be taken, with deadlines for implementation.

- Include only a very brief summary of discussions. Do not attribute comments to members, except possibly where formal motions are introduced (attribution for motions is not required). Meeting reports are not intended to document the discussion process, only the actions taken.

- Provide information on the time and place of the next meeting.

- Under some circumstances, especially where there are antitrust concerns, legal review of the meeting report may be required before distribution to committee members.

- Distribute the report to all committee members, including those who did not attend, immediately after the meeting, but certainly no later than two to three weeks after the meeting.

- In most instances, meeting reports do not require formal approval by the committee. The exception is formal meetings of an association's governing or management committees. A good approach for most committees is to send the meeting report out immediately after the meeting with instructions to contact the chair or staff liaison within a week if errors are noted. If necessary, a revised meeting report can then be distributed, noting that it is the Final Meeting Report. Do not waste time at subsequent meetings discussing, modifying, and approving minutes.

Follow-up After Meetings and Follow-through Between Meetings

- Create a tracking sheet that documents work to be done, by whom, and by what date. Periodically update it and send out between meetings.

- The chair should not take on tasks. Instead, he or she should delegate to others on the committee, and then spend time coordinating and tracking progress.

- Chair and staff liaison must agree as to who will make follow up contact to assure that interim committee work is being completed in a timely manner.

SAMPLE COMMITTEE REPORT FORM

I. Date

II. Committee

III. Committee Charge

IV. Committee Chair

V. Committee Members
   Board members

   Non-Board members

VI. Key Committee Activities—accomplishments and status of work in progress
   (Please provide in bullet point format)

VII. Board Action (check as appropriate)
   ___ No board action required
   ___ Board input is requested (please explain)

   ___ Board action is requested (please explain)

   ___ Committee recommendations to the board

COMMITTEE CHAIR/STAFF LIAISON PARTNERSHIP AGREEMENT

To be discussed, completed, and signed during the orientation program for the committee chair.

A strong partnership between volunteer leaders and staff liaisons is essential to assuring effective leadership, management, and productivity of committees. True partnerships are the result of mutual agreement as to roles, responsibilities, expectations, and commitments. To facilitate this, committee chairs and staff liaisons should start the year with agreement as to who will do what in managing and leading the committee throughout the year. This form is intended to assist in this process.

Committee _____

Committee chair _____

Phone _____   Fax _____

Email _____

Staff liaison _____

Phone _____   Fax_____

Email _____

Board liaison _____

Phone _____

Email _____

Agreements *(check or complete blanks where appropriate)*

1. ___ We have discussed and agree on the outcomes expected of this committee.

2. ___ We have discussed and agree on the manner in which the committee will conduct its work over the next year.

3. We agree to let no more than _____ hours pass without returning a phone call or email message from either of us.

4. _____ is responsible for developing the first draft of meeting agendas _____ days prior to each meeting.

5. Committee agendas will be sent to committee members no less than _____ days prior to face-to-face committee meetings or _____ days before conference calls.

6. _____ is responsible for taking notes during meetings, and _____ is responsible for drafting reports (minutes) of committee meetings and conference calls. Meeting reports will be approved by the chair within _____ days of receiving the draft report, and meeting reports will be distributed to all committee members no more than _____ days after the meeting/conference call.

7. _____ is responsible for drafting the committee report to the board, and the chair agrees to approve the draft report within _____ days of receipt if drafted by staff.

8. _____ is responsible for drafting all communications to the committee, and these will go out over the name of the (select one: chair, staff liaison, both).

9. Other agreements *(use reverse side)*

Chair's signature and date _____

Staff liaison's signature and date _____

Each person should tape a copy of this agreement to the inside cover of his/her committee file folder.

COMMITTEE FOCUS FOR THE YEAR

Effective committees are those that focus on achieving a limited number of outcomes directly linked to and supportive of achieving the association's strategic plan. To assist in assuring that the Committee remains focused, it is imperative that the Committee Chair and Staff Liaison agree on the key outcomes which the Committee is pursuing through its work, and this form is intended to assist in this process.

Committee _____

Committee chair _____

Staff liaison _____

Board liaison _____

List all objectives in the strategic plan that this committee's work is tied to.

List key outcomes the committee's work should focus on achieving this year.

1.

2.

3.

4.

List other committees, if any, in the association that are working in areas closely aligned with the work of this committee, and thus require coordination of work:

THE EFFECTIVE
COMMITTEE MEMBER

COMMITTEE MEMBER
POSITION DESCRIPTION

BASIC FUNCTION

Actively participate in the work of the committee; provide thoughtful input to the deliberations of the committee; focus on the best interests of the association and the committee rather than on personal or constituent interests; and work toward fulfilling the committee's goals.

RESPONSIBILITIES

- Review all relevant material before committee meetings. Make contributions and voice objective opinions on issues.
- Attend committee meetings.
- Carry out individual assignments made by the committee chair.
- Work as part of the committee and staff team to ensure that the committee proposes policies and/or develops products and services that help association members who are responsible for programs within the scope of interest of the committee.
- Represent the committee in meetings of other association groups.
- Promote clarity within the committee on the committee's role and how it supports and fits within the association.

ABOUT THE AUTHOR

John F. "Jack" Schlegel, PharmD, MSEd, CAE, is president of Schlegel & Associates, a consulting and training firm that assists association boards, volunteer leaders, and staff in improving leadership and governance for the purpose of achieving high performance. During his 17 years as an association executive, Dr. Schlegel served as the chief executive officer of three major national associations, including the now American Pharmacists Association. Previously he served on the faculty of the University of Southern California School of Pharmacy. Since forming Schlegel & Associates in 1994, he has worked with more than 300 associations, plus a number of universities and other organizations.

Jack holds B.S. and doctorate degrees in pharmacy, a fellowship in medical education, and a masters degree in higher education. He has received two honorary doctorates of science, has been awarded distinguished alumnus awards by his two alma maters, and has been listed in Who's Who for over 20 years. Jack has written over 100 articles and delivered hundreds of presentations on a broad range of topics in association management, health care, and public policy. He has also served as a director and officer on more than 30 governing boards.

EDUCATIONAL WORKSHOPS

Educational workshops on enhancing committee effectiveness are available for groups of staff and/or volunteer leaders. These are offered as two-hour, half-day, and full-day highly interactive training sessions. For more information please contact:

Schlegel & Associates
3390 Highlands Bridge Road
Sarasota, FL 34235 USA
JSchlegel@comcast.net
941-341-0434